National Board Certification®

Music: Early and Middle Childhood Exam Practice Questions

Mometrix
TEST PREPARATION

DEAR FUTURE EXAM SUCCESS STORY

First of all, **THANK YOU** for purchasing Mometrix study materials!

Second, congratulations! You are one of the few determined test-takers who are committed to doing whatever it takes to excel on your exam. **You have come to the right place.** We developed these practice tests with one goal in mind: to deliver you the best possible approximation of the questions you will see on test day.

Standardized testing is one of the biggest obstacles on your road to success, which only increases the importance of doing well in the high-pressure, high-stakes environment of test day. Your results on this test could have a significant impact on your future, and these practice tests will give you the repetitions you need to build your familiarity and confidence with the test content and format to help you achieve your full potential on test day.

Your success is our success

We would love to hear from you! If you would like to share the story of your exam success or if you have any questions or comments in regard to our products, please contact us at **800-673-8175** or **support@mometrix.com**.

Thanks again for your business and we wish you continued success!

Sincerely,
The Mometrix Test Preparation Team

Printed in the United States of America

TABLE OF CONTENTS

Practice Test #1

1. What is the mnemonic system that, when combined with hand motions, helps to reinforce the special relationship between pitches for sight-reading?

a. Roman numerals
b. C-clef
c. Solfege
d. Nashville system

2. What is the name of the soft tissue at the top of the mouth cavity that singers raise to produce a relaxed and free sound while also easing register transitions and maintaining the health of the vocal mechanisms?

a. Epiglottis
b. Velum
c. Pharynx
d. Uvula

3. Which of the following is the purpose of a *leitmotif*?

a. It musically represents a person, place, or idea.
b. It musically protests a political uprising.
c. It musically records the historic events of a place.
d. It musically inspires the audience to do a specific action.

4. The waltz is traditionally associated most with which time signature?

a. 2/2
b. 2/4
c. 4/4
d. 3/4

5. Instrumental warm-ups should:

a. Begin with the most challenging techniques to expedite the process.
b. Begin moderately then gradually increasing the speed, intensity, and range.
c. Begin and maintain slow tempo, low intensity, and a narrow range.
d. Begin with physical stretching and then proceed immediately to repertoire.

6. The Sugarhill Gang helped to widely popularize which term in their 1979 song *Rapper's Delight*?

a. Hip hop
b. Disco rap
c. Neo soul
d. Trip hop

7. Place the following brass instruments in order from brightest to darkest timbres: French horn, flugelhorn, trumpet, trombone.

a. Flugelhorn, trumpet, French horn, trombone
b. Trumpet, flugelhorn, trombone, French horn
c. Trombone, trumpet, flugelhorn, French horn
d. French horn, flugelhorn, trumpet, trombone

8. The rhythms of music are most related to:

a. The size of the canvas in a painting
b. The shape of a sculpture
c. The climax of the plot in a novel
d. The steps taken in dance

9. Which of the following philosophers in music education is most associated with aesthetic music education?

a. Edwin Gordon
b. Susanne Langer
c. Bennett Reimer
d. John Dewey

10. The black church heavily influenced which of the following musical genres through improvisation, storytelling, and call and response?

a. Metal
b. Latin
c. Grunge
d. Blues

11. A wind ensemble performs a piece in sonata form. How do they achieve beatless sonority when modulating?

a. Instruments performing the fundamental tones use a tuner to play with equal-tempered tuning, and other instruments compromise with embouchure adjustments and alternate fingerings to play with just intonation throughout the key changes.
b. Performers take into account that the equal-tempered tuning system is a compromise and that certain pitches and harmonies will naturally be slightly out-of-tune through key changes.
c. All instruments play with equal-tempered tuning in order to end the movement or piece on the same reference pitch within the key that the piece began.
d. Adjust the entire ensemble's reference pitches to equal temperament throughout the exposition, development, and recapitulation.

12. Which of the following is NOT an important element of an effective solo performance?

a. Dynamics
b. Correct intonation
c. Phrasing
d. Fingerings

13. Use the examples below to answer the following question.

Which of the following is a compound meter?

a. 

b. 

c. 

d. 

14. Which of the following articulations would best evoke a sense of raindrops?

a. Staccato
b. Legato
c. Tenuto
d. Fermata

15. How do sopranos maximize vocal tract resonance at high frequencies to achieve a vibrant sound?

a. By creating less space in the oral cavity and tightening the vocal tract
b. By creating more space in the oral cavity and relaxing the vocal tract
c. By creating less space in the oral cavity and relaxing the vocal tract
d. By creating more space in the oral cavity and tightening the vocal tract

16. Which of the following countries does the cajon come from?

a. Mexico
b. Mali
c. Peru
d. Jamaica

17. From which of the following countries does the mbira (finger piano) originate?

a. Zimbabwe
b. Japan
c. Peru
d. Chile

18. Which of the following would best help a music producer with career advancement in an increasingly competitive environment?

a. Increasing his or her social media output
b. Obtaining a master's degree in music
c. Buying the latest in audio technology
d. Diversifying his or her skill set

19. Which of the following tongue tension-releasing exercises best forms the basis for all exercises that help to release tension in the tongue?

a. Drinking lukewarm water to relax the tongue before vocalizing
b. Stretching the tongue using various techniques
c. Releasing tongue and jaw tension with massages and breathing exercises
d. Rolling the neck and head, keeping the mouth open and jaw down when rolling the head back

20. Use the example below to answer the question that follows.

Which of the following is the articulation that indicates the note is to be played at full length or slightly longer?

a. Accent
b. Staccato
c. Tenuto
d. Fermata

21. Which instrumentalist must be able to read the alto clef?

a. Oboe
b. Viola
c. Trombone
d. Baritone saxophone

22. Which of the following factors related to teaching to individual differences is most evident in the rating scale illustrated below?

Q&A Antecedent and Consequent Phrases Improvisation Rating Scale
1. Student responds, but the response is completely unmusical.
2. Student performs a song and a sense of melodic contour is evident. Student sings resting tone in tune. Does not demonstrate a sense of tonal syntax.
3. Student sings the resting tone and some pitches in tune, but does not sing tonal functions (e.g., V-I/IV-I or diatonic) that act as cadences in consequent phrases. Student demonstrates some sense of tonal syntax.
4. Student sings resting tone and some pitches in tune. Student sings a tonal function that can be included in a consequent phrase. Student demonstrates a sense of tonal syntax.
5. Student sings resting tone in tune and sings most tonal functions and pitches associated with a consequent phrase in tune. Student demonstrates a clear sense of tonal syntax by locking in tonality.
6. Student begins and ends in tune. Student sings all tonal functions and pitches associated with a consequent phrase in tune. Student demonstrates a clear sense of tonal syntax.

a. It is based upon the student responding with a consequent phrase.
b. It is a single-dimensional continuous rating scale.
c. The criteria within the rating scale are subjective.
d. Most students will score neither a 1 nor a 6.

23. Which of the following reasons for administering a music aptitude test is most appropriate for use in K–12 music education?

a. To use as tests for entrance into elite performance organizations
b. To assist in grading student achievement when compared to aptitude
c. To teach to students' individual strengths and weaknesses
d. To help students consider their choices when thinking about a career in music

24. When marking a music composition's form on a rehearsal/preparation score, which of the following rehearsal score preparation sequences is listed in the correct order when planning for ensemble rehearsals?

a. Determine form; mark motifs and phrases.
b. Mark large sections; mark periods and cadences.
c. Mark periods and cadences; mark motifs and phrases.
d. Mark large sections; determine form.

25. Ostinatos are found extensively in the music of which of the following countries?

a. China
b. Germany
c. Mexico
d. Ethiopia

26. Which of the following is the minimum appropriate performance duration for students performing grade level 4 band literature?

a. 9 minutes
b. 6 minutes
c. 10 minutes
d. 12 minutes

27. On reed instruments, reeds that are chipped or cracked should be:

a. Soaked
b. Discarded
c. Sanded
d. Trimmed

28. Use the example below to answer the question that follows.

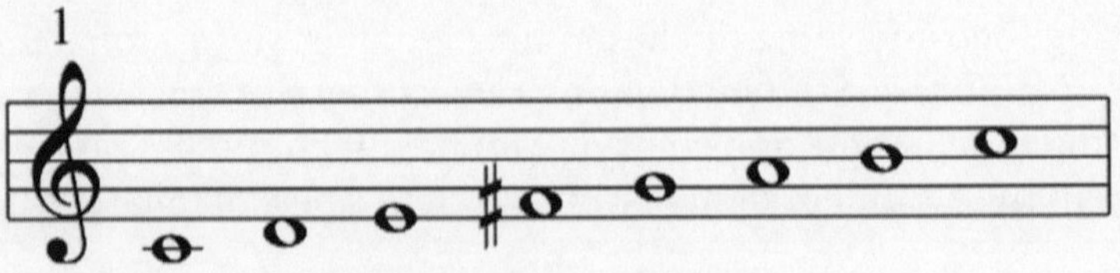

What is the musical mode shown in the example above?

a. Lydian
b. Dorian
c. Locrian
d. Phrygian

29. Which of the following jazz standards is performed in the bossa nova style?

a. "Desafinado"
b. "What Is This Thing Called Love"
c. "Cherokee"
d. "How High the Moon"

30. Which of the following is an example of *absolute music*, as opposed to *program music*?

a. *Symphony No. 5* by Ludwig van Beethoven
b. *Don Quixote* by Richard Strauss
c. *Danse Macabre* by Camille Saint-Saëns
d. *Symphonie Fantastique* by Hector Berlioz

31. Which of the following concert keys is a standard baritone saxophone pitched in?

a. Concert Bb
b. Concert Eb
c. Concert F
d. Concert G

32. How can conductors best promote cultural diversity in their music programs?

a. Take yearly trips to non-Western countries.
b. Include non-Western musical repertoire into concerts.
c. Have a non-Western music day camp.
d. Assign non-Western textbooks to all the students.

33. Which of the following careers is concerned with overseeing and promoting the health of the performing artist?

a. Critical care medicine
b. Music therapy
c. Medical nutrition therapy
d. Performing arts medicine

34. A beginning cello student plays with too much arm movement; what is most likely causing the problem?

a. The student's back is slouched.
b. The elbow is not bending properly on a bow stroke.
c. The thumb is placed too close to the second and third fingers.
d. The fingers are overly curved.

35. What physiological changes are happening to pubescent students when their voice "cracks"?

a. The pharynx expands and the uvula hardens.
b. The alveolar ridge thickens and the oral cavity widens.
c. The larynx enlarges and the vocal folds lengthen and thicken.
d. The glottis strengthens and hard palate lowers.

36. The Classical era and the Baroque era have distinct stylistic characteristics. Which of the following characteristics displayed in the following excerpt distinguishes it as a Baroque work?

(Bach's Brandenburg Concerto No. 1 in D Major, BWV 1046)

a. Figured bass
b. Changing mood
c. Balanced phrasing
d. Terraced dynamics

37. The twelve-tone technique of music was created by:

a. Anton Webern
b. Milton Babbit
c. Arnold Schoenberg
d. Pierre Boulez

38. Which of the following musical elements is a stylistic feature of the African musical tradition?

a. Dialogue
b. Modes
c. Discant
d. Coda

39. Which of the following reasons best explains why clarinets are tuned slightly sharp by the manufacturer?

a. Manufacturing the clarinet slightly sharp helps players perform all the tones throughout the register more closely to well-tempered tuning.
b. If a clarinet naturally plays flat with all joints pushed in, there is no easy remedy to put the instrument in tune.
c. Because there are options for purchasing shorter barrels based upon the manufacturer's design.
d. Performing slightly sharp is less abrasive on the listener's ear than performing flat.

40. Who of the following is credited with composing the following Requiem excerpt?

a. Wolfgang Mozart
b. Luigi Cherubini
c. Michael Haydn
d. Hector Berlioz

41. Which of the following marimba mallet grips provide the most independence for mallet movement?

a. Traditional crossed grip
b. Musser/Stevens grip
c. Two-mallet grip
d. Burton grip

42. Which of the following conducting patterns best fits the following music excerpt?

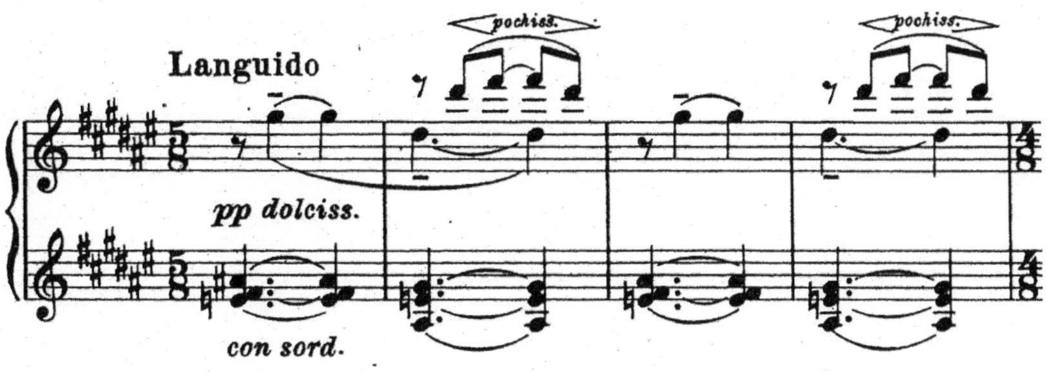

Scriabin Piano Sonata No. 5, Opus 53

a. 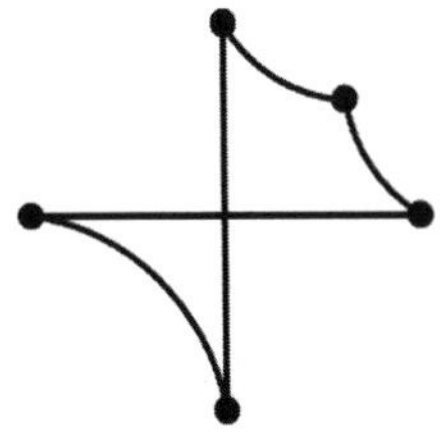

b. 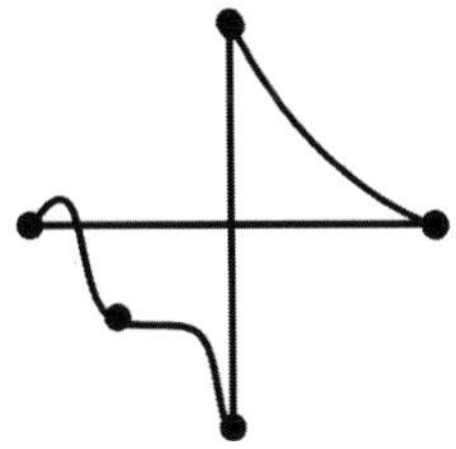

c. 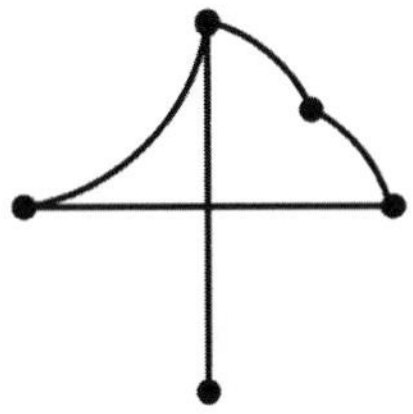

d. 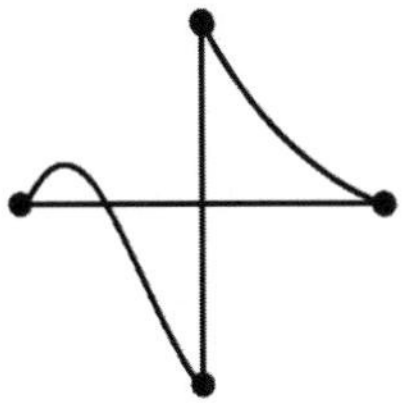

43. Which of the following Western music eras is this music excerpt from, and which genre does it represent?

a. Medieval; mass
b. Renaissance; motet
c. Renaissance; chanson
d. Baroque; cantata

44. What is the general range of the alto voice?

a. F3 to D5
b. C4 to A5
c. B2 to G4
d. E2 to C4

45. When beginning string players say their pegs do not hold, what is the most common cause?

a. They are not turning the pegs in a clockwise motion.
b. The length of the string is too long for the peg.
c. The instrument has entered an environment that is too humid.
d. They are not putting enough pressure on the end of the peg when turning it.

Answer Key and Explanations for Test #1

1. C: Solfege uses syllables that are assigned to the notes of a musical scale to aid musicians in mentally hearing the pitches of written music. Solfege should be reinforced by singing through a number of different keys to train the ears to hear the relationships between the diatonic pitches.

2. B: The soft tissue at the top of the mouth cavity that singers raise to produce a relaxed and free sound while also easing register transitions and maintaining the health of the vocal mechanisms is called the velum. When singers lift the soft palate, the resulting space within the oral cavity enlarges, helping to achieve a more resonant, warm tone without restrictions

3. A: The term *leitmotif* is used to identify a reoccurring motivic fragment that musically represents some part of a musical drama, usually a person, place, or idea. The leitmotif is a useful tool for composers: character development, the unfolding of the story, reinforcement of the action taking place onstage, and recalling an event or person from a previous scene are all techniques of the leitmotif.

4. D: The 3/4 time signature means that there are three beats to each measure, and the quarter note equals one beat. A way to make 3/4, or waltz time, easy to hear is to count, "*One* two three, *one* two three" repeatedly, stressing the first beat. 2/2 (A), or cut time, means there are two beats to each measure, and the half note equals one beat. In 2/4 (B) time, there are two beats to every measure, and the quarter note equals one beat. In 4/4 (C) time, there are four beats to a measure, and the quarter note equals one beat. Waltz time has three counts per measure, rather than an even number (2 or 4) like the others.

5. B: Instrumental warm-ups should begin moderately then gradually increase the speed, intensity, and range. The warm-up promotes blood flow to the entire body, lubricating all music-making muscles and joints. Starting moderately and increasing the speed, intensity, and range helps to prepare both the player and the instrument.

6. A: In their 1979 hit single *Rapper's Delight*, The Sugarhill Gang helped to popularize the term "hip hop" into mainstream culture. The lyrics read: "I said a hip hop, hippie to the hippie, the hip, hip a hop, and you don't stop, a rock it to the bang bang boogie, say, up jump the boogie, to the rhythm of the boogie, the beat."

7. B: These are the brass instruments given in order from brightest to darkest timbres: trumpet, flugelhorn, trombone, and French horn. The size and aspect of the conical bore affects the instrument's timbre, and of the four instruments, trumpets have the narrowest and most cylindrical bore, while the French horn has the widest and biggest bore.

8. D: The rhythms of music are most related to the steps taken in dance. The size of canvas in a painting would relate more to the length or orchestration of a piece, the shape of a sculpture would relate more to the structure of a musical piece, and the climax of the plot in a novel would relate more to the climax of music.

9. C: Reimer's famous book about the "feelingfulness" of music and music education became popular during the 1960s through 1980s in music education, and was later challenged by the philosophies of Edwin Gordon, who focused more on audiation. Aesthetic music education is still a cornerstone for music education and music education classes that introduce music education philosophy to future music teachers.

10. D: Blues music was heavily influenced by the black church through improvisation, storytelling, call and response, vocal inflections, and the blues progression. Many of these musical features are now representative of the blues genre of music.

11. A: Because sonata form modulates to different keys (and tonalities), if the ensemble is to perform using beatless just intonation, it is impossible for all instrumentalists to perform to their own instrument's compromised tuning system, which resembles as close as possible the compromise of equal temperament made among the 12 tones that instrument manufacturers make. Also, because sonata form ends in the original key, it is important for ensembles to avoid straying too far from equal temperament in order to end a piece with the same fundamental reference pitches in the original key. Thus, it is important for instrumentalists who play the fundamental tones within a key (e.g., the tonic) to stay as close to equal temperament as possible throughout key and tonality changes, while other players compromise and adjust to the changes throughout. In the end, it must be acknowledged that tuning is a matter of compromise in order to perform beatless harmonies.

12. D: Of the given answer choices, fingerings are not an important element of an effective solo performance. Fingerings are a useful tool for playing passages efficiently and with ease. However, without dynamics, correct intonation, and tasteful phrasing, the essence of the music will not be effectively conveyed to an audience.

13. D: In compound meter, the number of pulses can be subdivided into groups of three. Of the answer choices, only answer D can be subdivided into two groups of three. All the other options are examples of simple meters (simple duple, simple triple, simple quadruple).

14. A: The staccato articulation would best evoke a sense of raindrops, with its short and light sound texture. A legato articulation is smooth and connected, unlike the short drops of rain. A tenuto articulation is held longer than a staccato and would also not represent raindrops as well. A fermata articulation means to hold a note for an extended period of time.

15. B: Many sopranos will maximize vocal tract resonance at high frequencies by creating more space in the oral cavity and relaxing the vocal tract so that the resultant sound is vibrant and sonorous. The vocal tract has optimal resonances for certain frequencies, and it is important for the singer to maximize the resonances of the vibrating vocal tract with the specific pitch frequencies.

16. C: The cajon is a wooden box percussion instrument. Peruvian slaves from West Africa created it using packing crates to replace the percussion instruments that they left behind. Western pop music has adopted the use of the cajon. Drummers can now be seen performing pop songs while sitting on a cajon and beating Western rhythm to pop music.

17. A: The mbira originates from Zimbabwe. The mbira is a wooden box with strips of metal attached in a way that the player can pluck them with their fingers to produce different notes. The mbira has also been used by the US band Earth, Wind & Fire.

18. D: Diversifying his or her skill set would best help a music producer with career advancement in an increasingly competitive environment. Although increasing social media marketing, having the latest audio technology, and having a master's degree in music may help somewhat, being able to perform as many skills as possible would best help a music producer with career advancement.

19. B: Tongue stretching exercises include sticking out the tongue in various directions as far as possible, then relaxing; yawning while producing a soft-sounding siren, which allows the tongue to come out and down; stretching the tongue out and down to produce a circle of sound that cannot be broken if the tongue is relaxed; and placing the tip of the tongue at the bottom of the front teeth and arching the tongue forward so that the back of the tongue can be felt (this exercise can also be done when placing a curl within the tongue while phonating). Options A, C, and D are all other techniques to improve vocalization by relaxing the tongue, but tongue stretches are paramount.

20. C: When an accent mark is present, it means to play with stress on that note. Staccato means to play with a shortened sound duration. Fermata means to hold a note longer than written, customarily up to twice as long as normal. The correct answer is tenuto, which means to play at full length or slightly longer. Both fermata and tenuto indicate that a musical element should be lengthened; however, a fermata usually indicates a longer pause than tenuto.

21. B: The oboe uses the treble clef. The tenor trombone uses the bass and tenor clefs. The Eb baritone saxophone uses the treble clef but sounds an octave and a major sixth lower than what is read. Parts for the viola are typically written in the alto clef, so violists must be able to read this clef.

22. D: Option D is the correct answer because teachers do not want a floor or ceiling effect when working to teach to individual strengths and weakness. An arbitrary point that demonstrates minimal competency can be established at any point along the rating scale, and grades can also be arbitrarily derived along the continuum of the rating scale.

If, for example, a student scored a 6 on this ratings scale, there would be no room for that student to grow, and the teacher could not identify individual strengths and weaknesses in order to help the student improve his musicianship. Option B is incorrect because, while this is a single-dimensional rating scale, that alone does not help to teach to individual differences.

Performances that require the use of multiple rating scales (e.g., tonal, rhythmic, and expressive) can employ multiple judges in order to avoid the halo effect and so that each rating scale can be properly attended to. Or, one judge can record the performance anonymously (to avoid bias) and rate the performance for each rating scale 5-10 days apart. This takes time, but measurement and evaluation of student achievement have become high stakes. Thus, properly measuring performances is integral to the teaching and learning process and is the primary component of the teaching and learning process in evidence-centered design.

23. C: Students have an inherent right to learn and be accommodated to their individual strengths and weaknesses. Options A, B, and D may all be used by teachers and students. However, because no test by itself is a perfect representation of a student's potential, along with other considerations, these options are either ancillary or ethically questionable.

24. D: When using a rehearsal/preparation score, the appropriate sequence for understanding a composition's form is described below in the fifth step for working with a rehearsal/preparation score for teaching and conducting.

The steps to using a rehearsal score are enumerated below.

1. Number measures.
2. If a choral piece, whisper through the text. If the text is foreign, write the literal translation down.
3. Play at the piano and sing every individual part.
4. Analyze/audiate the harmonic content.
5. Mark the form, beginning with motifs and phrases. Mark periods and cadences. Proceed to large sections. Determine form.

6. Mark expressive elements, including dynamics and dynamic terminology, articulation marks.
7. Play or finger through every part on every instrument.
8. Mark technically difficult material.
9. Create measurable learning objectives and concomitant performance rating scales.
10. Reduce the score at the piano.
11. Create an interpretation chart.
    - Where to stagger breathing
    - How to turn/shape phrases
    - Tempo/rubato/caesura
    - Music history lessons
    - Music theory lessons
    - Audiation lessons
12. Listen to the piece, preferably more than one recording. Listen last to avoid undue influence by other interpretations.

25. D: An ostinato is defined as a short, repeating accompaniment pattern throughout a musical work that can consist of a simple rhythmic, melodic, or harmonic idea. Similar to a drone, the ostinato provides a stable foundation for the main melody line. Ostinatos are found extensively in sub-Saharan African world music, including Ethiopian music.

26. B: A six-minute performance duration is reflected in the body of literature for grade level 4 works for band, and it is the suggested time length for the American Band College Music Grading Chart. It is interesting to note that grade level 4 music is shorter in duration than grade 3. This is because of the extended range and endurance required for performing without rest.

27. B: On reed instruments, reeds that are chipped or cracked should be discarded. There is usually not a way to repair chipped or cracked reeds. Players should always keep spare reeds nearby for backup and practice proper reed maintenance to prolong the life of each reed.

28. A: The mode in the given example is most related to the C major scale, indicated by the major third interval (C to E) and the major sixth and seventh intervals (C to A and C to B, respectively). Of the answer choices, the Lydian mode, answer A is most similar to the major scale, with a raised fourth degree—F# in the example. Dorian, Locrian, and Phrygian modes are most similar to the minor scale.

29. A: "Desafinado," composed by Antonio Carlos Jobim, with lyrics created by Newton Mendonça, is a song in the bossa nova style, and the title means "out of tune" or "off key." The bossa nova style originated in Brazil in the early 1950s and is a subgenre of samba (a Latin dance subgenre), much like bebop is a subgenre of jazz music.

It's helpful to understand the bossa nova style in relation to its origins in samba. The samba is a subgenre of Latin music that is as much social as it is about musical factors. Samba lyrics speak about collective life, particular notable events, persons, and culture. Samba first appeared in Bahia, Brazil, and was known as the music of slaves.

Musically, the samba is usually played with guitar, bass, and drums. It can include other instruments, including orchestral instruments. The samba is livelier than the bossa nova, but is harmonically simpler, with fewer chord extensions and less complex voicings. Bossa nova uses major and minor seventh and 13th chords and is usually softer and smoother in style and sound.

It's generally not danced to as the samba is because it has no formal dance steps. Bossa nova is usually slower in tempo than the samba.

Bossa nova is highbrow samba. Its lyrics are more about the individual and the topic is often about love, loneliness, or living a pleasurable life. The singing voice is less formal and opera-like than samba.

30. A: Absolute music is defined as instrumental music that exists apart from extra-musical references. Programmatic music is music that can be represented by non-musical images or ideas. Of the answer choices, only answer A, *Symphony No. 5* by Ludwig van Beethoven, exists apart from extra-musical references.

31. B: A standard baritone saxophone is pitched in concert Eb. The baritone saxophone sounds an octave plus a major sixth lower than written. Modern baritones with a low A key and high F♯ key have a range from C2 to A4.

32. B: Conductors can promote cultural diversity in their music programs by including non-Western musical repertoire into their concerts. Although yearly international trips may sound appealing, it is neither practical nor cost-effective. Neither devoting only a day to non-Western music nor assigning textbooks to students effectively promotes cultural diversity within a music program.

33. D: Performing arts medicine is concerned with overseeing and promoting the health of the performing artist. Medical health professionals evaluate and treat any medical problems that may occur in the performing artist. The focus is to prevent re-injury, and treatment may also cover technique, repertoire, instrument state, and emotional state adjustments, as related to the injury.

34. B: A beginning cello student who plays with too much arm movement is most likely not bending the elbow properly on a bow stroke. When bowing on a cello, students should use not only their upper arms, but also their forearms, elbows, wrists, hands, and fingers as well. A stiff elbow causes too much arm movement during a bow stroke.

35. C: Voice development will affect vocal students as the larynx enlarges and the vocal folds lengthen and thicken. The physiological changes of the vocal mechanisms tend to affect boys more than girls, evident in the "cracking" of the voice. During puberty, students will have to work towards singing voice production, pitch accuracy, and increasing vocal range.

36. D: Dynamics refer to how volume changes in a piece. In this excerpt, terraced dynamics are created by the sudden changing texture of the music. Figured bass is a defining characteristic of the Baroque era, but it is not used in this excerpt. Changing mood and balanced phrasing are more associated with the Classical era and not the Baroque.

37. C: Arnold Schoenberg developed the twelve-tone technique of music in which all twelve pitches of the chromatic scale are treated as equal. Anton Webern, Milton Babbit, and Pierre Boulez were composers who subsequently used the twelve-tone technique in their compositions, but they did not create it.

38. A: Dialogue, also known as call and response, is an important stylistic element of the African musical tradition. The call and response form has been widely influential in music such as blues, jazz, hip hop, rock, and gospel. Modes can be traced to the ancient Greek tradition, discant is an element of Medieval music, and coda refers to musical form within Western classical music.

39. B: There is one remedy for a clarinet that plays flat, and it is costly: purchasing a shorter barrel. Therefore, clarinets are typically tuned slightly sharp by the manufacturer.

40. A: This Requiem excerpt was composed by Wolfgang Mozart. Mozart was almost certainly influenced by Michael Haydn's *Requiem*. In turn, Hector Berlioz's *Dies Irae* is said to rival the magnificence of Mozart's *Requiem*. Robert Schumann proclaimed Cherubini's (a contemporary of Mozart) *Requiem* as being "without equal," and Beethoven requested that Cherubini's be played at his own funeral.

41. B: The Musser/Stevens marimba mallet grip provides the most independence for mallet movement. It places the first mallet between the thumb and index fingers, and the second mallet between the middle and ring fingers so that the mallets are not crossed.

42. B: Scriabin's (1871-1915) fifth piano sonata was composed in 1907, and the above excerpt is the second theme. The music is marked *Languido*, which means sluggish, spiritless. The bass clef provides the best direction for conducting, as it is in a 3+2 pattern, and the music is slow enough so that the treble clef can easily follow this pattern. Option A is a 4+1 pattern. Option C is a 1+4 pattern. Option D is a 2+3 pattern.

43. B: This motet is titled *Acceptit Jesus calicem*, by Giovanni Palestrina (1525 A.D.-1594 A.D.). This late Renaissance motet is characterized by its:

- Highly polyphonic nature, with each line being of equal importance
- Imitative quality
- Having Latin text
- Being sacred (although some motets, beginning in the high Medieval period, were composed about courtly love). This motet is based upon "our father," beginning with "*pater noster*." This is in contrast to the mass, which had five parts: Kyrie, Gloria, Credo, Sanctus, Agnus Dei
- Still being relatively modal
- Containing a cantus firmus
- Small jumps, and a stepwise move in the opposite direction after a jump
- Notation that is developed beyond the notation of the Medieval period, and all of the parts are on one sheet of paper
- Characteristic complex music that overtakes the text
- Fluid style rather than static in movement
- Dissonances that are confined to suspensions

44. A: The general vocal range of the alto voice is from F3 to D5. The general vocal range of the soprano voice is from C4, middle C, to A5; the general vocal range of the tenor voice is from B2 to G4; and the general vocal range of the bass voice is from E2 to C4. Although many composers use these ranges in writing a piece of four-part harmony, each individual's voice can vary drastically in range and ability.

45. D: When beginning string players say their pegs do not hold, the most common cause is that they are not putting enough pressure on the end of the peg when turning it. Correctly winding the strings on the pegs is very important for the pegs to work correctly. Students should imagine the peg as having screw threads with which to wind the peg.

Practice Test #2

1. Use the example below to answer the question that follows.

Which of the following is the name of the note in the above example?

a. C-sharp
b. E-sharp
c. A-sharp
d. G-sharp

2. Which of the following is NOT an example of compound musical form?

a. Sonata form
b. Binary form
c. Minuet and trio
d. Rondo form

3. For valved brass instruments that are used nearly daily, how often should valve oil be applied?

a. Only in particularly dry conditions
b. When storing the instrument long-term
c. Two to three times per week
d. After an extended performance

4. Reggae music originated in which Caribbean nation in the 1960s?

a. Haiti
b. Cuba
c. Trinidad
d. Jamaica

5. How did the orchestra shift the way it used certain instrument families from the Baroque to the Classical era?

a. Violins became the dominant string section, while the lower strings became the supporting background.
b. Strings and winds were doubled on every thematic line.
c. Bassoons became part of the supporting bass texture.
d. Woodwinds became the prominent rhythmic support section, while strings played secondary rhythmic roles.

6. Which of the following musical terms comes from the Italian term meaning "to hurry"?

a. *Slentando*
b. *Allargando*
c. *Affrettando*
d. *Calando*

7. A performer's decision to add dramatic intent within a certain musical piece is conceptually most similar to:

a. A painter's decision to use white instead of black paint
b. An actor's personal interpretation of character lines
c. A writer's alternate ending of a novel
d. A dancer's warm-up before a debut performance

8. Which of the following typically describes rondo form?

a. AABBCC
b. ABBAB
c. ABACABA
d. AABA

9. The structure of sonata form in music is most similar to which literary narrative structure?

a. Setup – bridge – resolution
b. Setup – plot – conflict
c. Setup – conflict – resolution
d. Setup – resolution – plot

10. Which of the following is the earliest form of jazz music?

a. West Coast jazz
b. Kansas City blues
c. Latin jazz
d. New Orleans jazz

11. Which of the following is an example of *leitmotif*?

a. The distinctive, repetitive change from E to F in John Williams' theme for Jaws
b. Pieces in which an orchestra accompanies a harpsichord, as composed by Bach
c. The challenging key changes in César Franck's Symphony in D minor
d. The book containing the words to Giuseppe Verdi's *La Traviata*

12. Use the example below to answer the question that follows.

The bass in the above example uses which of the following rhythmic patterns?

a. 3-2 clave
b. Ostinato
c. Bossa nova
d. Alberti bass

13. Which of the following range(s) do most double horn players use the Bb side of the instrument for?

a. Middle register, from C4 to C5
b. Upper register, from C#5 to C6
c. Lower and middle registers, from C3 to C5
d. Lower, middle, and upper registers, from C3 to F3 and G#4 to C6.

14. Taking in a deep breath over as many counts as possible, holding the breath, and then slowly letting out the air on an "S" sound, over as many counts as possible, is an example of what kind of vocal warm-up?

a. Octave warm-up
b. Falsetto warm-up
c. Tessitura warm-up
d. Breathing warm-up

15. Vocal resonance is important for an effective vocal solo performance because:

a. It increases breathing capacity.
b. It simulates harmonic overtones.
c. It creates a well-projected sound.
d. It clarifies vocal diction.

16. How should a conductor's elbow generally be positioned?

a. Raised high above the podium
b. Close to the torso
c. Pointed to the front of the ensemble
d. Slightly raised away from the body

17. What is a benefit of having sectional rehearsals as opposed to having only full rehearsals?

a. The players have to clean, adjust, and tune their instruments together.
b. The players are able to work out their counterpoint on original compositions.
c. The players have the opportunity to work on their sight-reading skills.
d. The players are able to fine-tune their parts together.

18. Musical phrasing, contour, and line can be most analogous to:

a. The choice of subject and medium in a painting
b. The synchrony and interaction between dancers in a ballet
c. The melding of flavors and ingredients in culinary arts
d. The cadence and inflection of language in a narrated text

19. What is the name of that range within a singer's vocal abilities that resonates in the most aesthetically pleasing manner and is usually the most comfortable to sing?

a. Chest voice
b. Tessitura
c. Falsetto
d. Register

20. Which of the following was an early form of polyphony during the Medieval period in which voices were sung in parallel motion?

a. Motet
b. Gregorian chant
c. Mass
d. Organum

21. Which movement in music paralleled the movement in visual arts led by painters such as Monet, Cézanne, Degas, Manet, and Renoir?

a. Impressionism
b. Rococo
c. Neoclassicism
d. Abstraction

22. Which of the following composers wrote an opera based upon Shakespeare's *Othello*?

a. Verdi
b. Puccini
c. Berlioz
d. Handel

23. Use the example below to answer the question that follows.

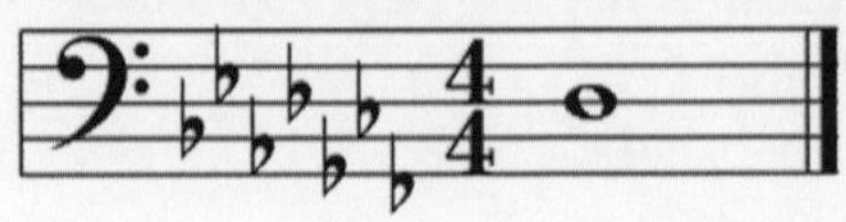

Which of the following is the name of the note in the above example?

a. B-flat
b. D
c. B
d. D-flat

24. Which major pedagogue developed the system of music education through movement called eurythmics?

a. Kodály
b. Dalcroze
c. Orff
d. Suzuki

25. Given the following music excerpt, which of the following saxophone fingerings for Bb is most appropriate for fingering the Bb in the first measure?

a. 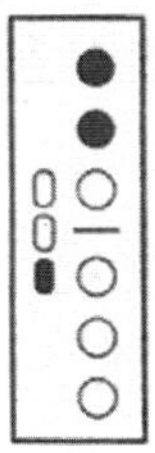

b. 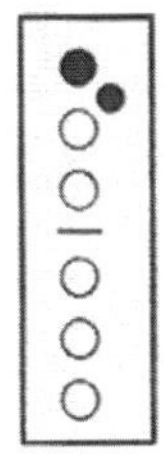

c. 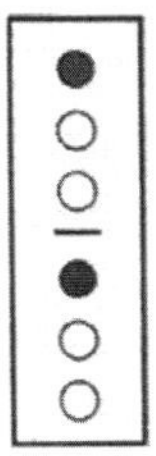

d. 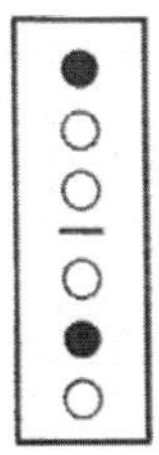

26. Competitions for chair positions in a student band or orchestra:

a. should be held daily
b. have no place in the rehearsal space of a music educator in charge of developing musicians' self-esteem
c. should be held at the beginning and end of the semester only
d. should be held both unannounced and on a scheduled basis, at the instructor's discretion

27. The jazz improvisational style can be most closely compared to what Classical musical style?

a. Baroque music
b. Minimalist music
c. Symphonic music
d. Impressionist music

28. Of the following, which is the most secure job in music, providing extensive opportunities to tour, record, and perform at high-profile ceremonies as well as college repayment, health care, and other benefits?

a. Cruise ship musician
b. Orchestra musician
c. Military musician
d. Band musician

29. The Middle Eastern *maqam* system of melodic organization is most similar to which aspect of Western music theory?

a. Counterpoint
b. Binary form
c. Modes
d. Notation

30. Which of the following "Mighty Five" compositional techniques is used in the following music excerpt?

(Mussorgsky, *Pictures at an Exhibition*, "Promenade")

a. Modular rotation
b. Heterophony
c. Whole-tone scale
d. Octatonic scale

31. What is NOT an aspect of the score the conductor needs to learn when preparing a score?

a. Form
b. Transpositions
c. Publisher
d. Dynamics

32. Which of the following composers wrote the famous melody seen in the lower strings of the following music excerpt?

a. Mozart
b. Mahler
c. Beethoven
d. Schubert

33. Use the example below to answer the question that follows.

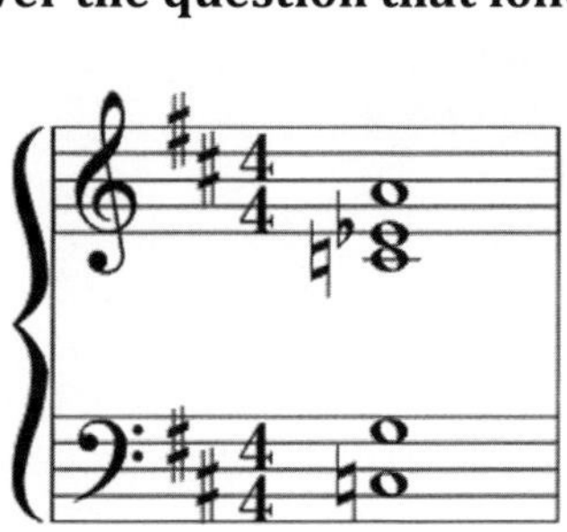

Name the harmony in the above example.

a. C°7
b. Aø7
c. G °7
d. Eb ø7

34. Use the example below to answer the question that follows.

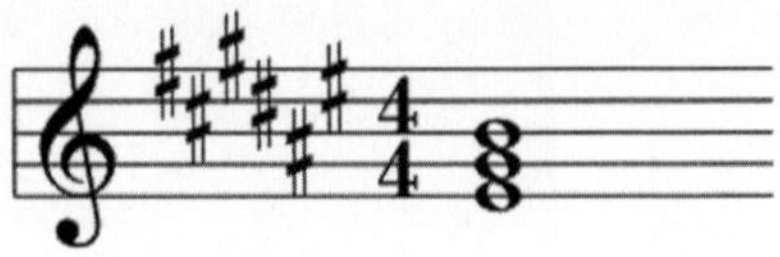

The chord in the above example can be best described as which of the following?

a. vii°
b. V
c. ii
d. iv

35. Which of the following regions of the world does the gamelan come from?

a. Pakistan
b. Indonesia
c. China
d. Australia

36. Which of the following concert pitches should sound when playing on the clarinet barrel and mouthpiece alone?

a. F#
b. Bb
c. Ab
d. E

37. Use the example below to answer the question that follows.

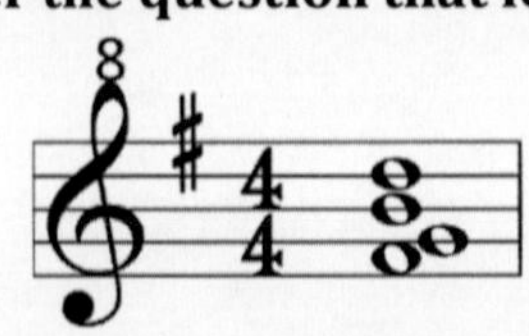

Which of the following best describes the seventh chord in the above example?

a. Major seventh in third inversion
b. Dominant seventh in second inversion
c. Major/minor seventh in third inversion
d. Minor seventh in second inversion

38. Which of the following is the most fundamental tool for beginning improvisation?

a. Syncopation
b. Imitation
c. Modulation
d. Inversion

39. How often should a conductor check for accurate intonation of the ensemble?

a. Only at the beginning of rehearsals
b. Every third rehearsal
c. Periodically during rehearsals
d. At the end of every rehearsal

40. A loud, forceful, and fast sound tends to convey which of the following moods?

a. Sorrow
b. Calm
c. Hope
d. Passion

41. Which of the following compositional tools describes a group of closely spaced notes played simultaneously, usually in intervals of adjacent seconds and groupings?

a. Extended harmony
b. Tone cluster
c. Diminished seventh
d. Retrograde inversion

42. What is the name of the playing technique for French horn that produces a slightly darker tone, more easily controls pitch, and aids in performing extended techniques such as stopped horn and echo horn?

a. Left-hand technique
b. Open-fist technique
c. Hand-horn technique
d. Closed-throat technique

43. Which of the following is NOT a double reed woodwind instrument?

a. Oboe
b. Bassoon
c. Clarinet
d. Sarrusophone

44. Which opera form of the Enlightenment featured three acts with alternating arias and recitatives with usually six or seven characters?

a. Opera buffa
b. Opera comique
c. Opera seria
d. Opera greco

45. A career in music business would include which of the following job titles?

a. Composer
b. Publicist
c. Accompanist
d. Vocalist

Answer Key and Explanations for Test #2

1. C: In the treble clef, the lines from bottom to top are: E, G, B, D, F. From the fifth line on the treble clef, the first ledger line above that is an interval of one-third higher. Because the top line is F, an interval of a third up would be A. The correct answer, then, is A#.

2. B: Compound musical form describes a tonal work that can be seen as a composite of other, smaller, simple forms such as binary and ternary forms. Sonata form, minuetto and trio, and rondo form are all composed of multiple distinct sections or movements. The only answer choice that is not a compound form is binary form, answer choice B.

3. C: For valved brass instruments, a small amount of valve oil should be applied a few times a week or before each playing session to prevent parts from seizing. Clean and lubricate all slides, removing old lubricant before applying a new layer, and use only a small amount, removing any excess with a soft cloth. Brass instruments should not be over-oiled, but they do generally need frequent oiling with use. Depending on the player and the instrument, an instrument may even need to be oiled daily or even in the middle of a longer performance.

4. D: Reggae music originated in the Caribbean nation of Jamaica in the 1960s. The music has roots in traditional calypso and mento music as well as in American jazz, rhythm and blues, ska, and the rocksteady movement of the 60s. Early Jamaican reggae musicians include Jackie Mittoo, Winston Wright, "Scratch" Perry, and The Pioneers.

5. A: In the Baroque era, strings and winds were often doubled to play certain lines. With the new Classical era, first violins were the dominant string section, while the lower strings became the supporting background harmonically and rhythmically. The bassoon became increasingly independent as opposed to the previous Baroque setting of the bassoon as part of the bass line.

6. C: The answer choices all have to do with a change in tempo; however, only one indicates a quickening of the tempo. *Affrettando*, the correct answer, comes from Italian, meaning "to hurry." *Slentando* also comes from Italian, meaning "to slow down;" *allargando* comes from Italian, meaning "to widen;" and *calando* comes from Italian, meaning "to let down."

7. B: A performer's decision to add dramatic intent within a certain musical piece is conceptually most similar to an actor's personal interpretation of character lines. Just as a performer chooses how to interpret the dynamics and markings of a musical work, an actor similarly chooses how to deliver the lines of his or her character.

8. C: Rondo form is defined by a principal theme (A) in the tonic key that alternates with episodes (B and C). The five-part rondo is usually described as ABACA. The 7-part rondo is usually described as ABACABA, which is answer C. Answer A describes chain form. Answer B is not a generally recognized musical form. Answer D is ternary form.

9. C: The structure of sonata form features three main sections: exposition, development, and recapitulation. This is similar to the setup, conflict, and resolution of literary narrative structure. In both the setup and exposition, the main idea is introduced. In the development and conflict, the melody and plot lines progress. In the recapitulation and resolution, both melody and plot lines resolve at the end.

10. D: New Orleans jazz, developed at the start of the 20th century, was one of the earliest forms of jazz music, borrowing from the music of black and creole musicians. West Coast jazz was developed in the 1950s, Kansas City blues was developed in the 1920s and 1930s, and Latin jazz was developed in the 1940s and 1950s.

11. A: The distinctive music used for the movie *Jaws* whenever the shark appears or is nearby. By definition, a *leitmotif* is a distinctive musical theme or melody associated with a particular story element such as a character or place. The shark's theme in *Jaws* would be a classic example. Answers B through D describe the terms *concerto, chromatic modulation,* and *libretto,* respectively.

12. B: In the given example, the bass repeats a rhythmic pattern on the same note, similarly to a drone. This is an example of a rhythmic ostinato, a short, constantly repeating rhythmic pattern. A 3-2 clave would have a rhythm of three followed by a rhythm of two, a bossa nova is also a specific rhythmic pattern that would be repeated in different harmonies, and an Alberti bass refers to a bass figuration that outlines the tones within a triad.

13. B: The Bb side of the horn is smaller, causing the partials to be further apart in the beginning range and making it easier for beginners to hit the correct notes. Most double horn players use it primarily in the upper register. The Bb side of the horn is engaged by pressing the thumb trigger. Although the fingerings for the F side and the Bb side are mostly different, each side is read with the same notation and sounds the same for each notated note. Because the horn has both the F and Bb sides, and because pitch tendencies associated with the slides and valve combinations make intonation somewhat difficult throughout the register, players can make slight adjustments to pitches with their hand in the bell (the further in, the lower the pitch) and with their embouchure.

14. D: This is an example of a breathing warm-up. Breathing warm-ups engage the diaphragm for supported singing and help to warm the vocal cords for singing.

15. C: Vocal resonance is important for an effective vocal solo performance because it creates a well-projected sound. Singing in the proper vocal register without strain, with strong vocal cords, and with the tongue and mouth in position to maximize resonance helps to project the singing voice.

16. D: A conductor's elbow should be positioned so that it is slightly raised away from the body. The baton can then be best and clearly seen from all angles. It should not be raised high above the podium, close to the torso, nor pointed to the front of the ensemble; the baton should be a natural extension of the hand and arm.

17. D: Sectional rehearsals allow players to fine-tune their parts together and to fix any technical or musical problems apart from the full ensemble. Sometimes, the conductor may not be aware of other hidden problems except through listening to sectional rehearsals.

18. D: Musical phrasing, contour, and line can be most analogous to the cadence and inflection of language in a narrated text. Many musical analogies relate to the spoken word, such as "call and response" or "question and answer." Musical phrasing, contour, and line are all found in the cadence of language.

19. B: Tessitura refers to that range within a singer's vocal abilities that resonates in the most aesthetically pleasing manner and that is generally the most comfortable for the singer. Tessitura differs from vocal range in that the range of a singer's voice refers to the limits of pitches the singer is able to sing.

20. D: Organum is an early form of polyphony developed during the Medieval period in which voices were sung in parallel motion. The motet evolved from organum and featured a tenor line with contrasting upper voices. Gregorian chant has melodies with no meter, and masses are large-scale works that also feature polyphony in counterpoint.

21. A: The Impressionist music movement of the 19th and 20th centuries paralleled the visual arts movement of Édouard Manet, Claude Monet, Edgar Degas, Pierre-Auguste Renoir, Berthe Morisot, Camille Pissarro, Alfred Sisley, and Mary Cassatt. Both painters and composers abandoned formal elements and created works that caught the soft, brief, and sensory effects of a particular moment.

22. A: Verdi's opera *Otello* premiered in 1887 and was based on Shakespeare's *Othello*. It was Verdi's second-to-last opera. Gioachino Rossini also wrote a well-known opera called *Otello*, but his version was not based on Shakespeare's *Othello*.

23. D: The note in the example is D-flat. The key signature contains seven flats: Bb, Eb, Ab, Db, Gb, Cb, and Fb; therefore, the answer can be neither choice B nor choice C. The third line of the bass clef is a D, but the key signature indicates that this should be a D-flat; a careless error may result in reading the third line as B, which is only valid in the treble clef.

24. B: The system of music education through movement called eurythmics was developed around 1900 by Swiss composer, musician, and pedagogue Émile Jaques-Dalcroze, in which students use a kinesthetic approach to experience musical concepts. The body is seen as the instrument, and students discover musicality, tempo, dynamics, and phrase structure through physical dialogue with the music.

25. A: Two essential rules for woodwind fingerings are:

1. Don't slide fingers

2. Don't lift fingers on one hand while pressing fingers on the other hand

Choices C and D would require lifting up a finger on the left hand while placing a finger down with the right hand, then doing the opposite after leaving the Bb. Choice B would require sliding with the fingers of the left hand.

26. D: Competitions for chair placement should be held both with advance notice and at unannounced times. Periodic competitions for first chair and so on keep more advanced students playing at their best level; many students further down the row will strive to improve their play in order to catch up. The result is a better orchestra. Therefore, answer B is incorrect; while a student's self-esteem is important, all musicians should be able to withstand the pressure of demonstrating their skills to their peers and their instructor. Accordingly, both announced and unannounced competitions have their place in this process. Daily competitions, answer A, would obviously be excessive in a student orchestra's busy schedule. Answer C, conversely, would not put *enough* motivation or pressure on the students to improve.

27. A: Of the given answer choices, the best answer is Baroque music. Baroque music was traditionally improvised, as in jazz music, and followed a standard in performance, whether a 32-bar form in jazz or a ritornello form in Baroque music. In both genres, improvisations are based on outlined chord symbols that direct the melody.

28. C: Military musicians have the most secure job in music, with extensive opportunities to tour, record, and perform at high-profile ceremonies as well as college repayment, health care, and other benefits. The Army, Navy, Air Force, and Coast Guard all have full-time music ensembles. Ensembles are characterized as either premier bands or regional bands.

29. C: The *maqam* system of melodic organization used in Middle Eastern music most resembles the Western mode. There are more than 30 different *maqamat*, and each defines the melodic contour, pitches, and hierarchical development of the scale.

30. A: Modular rotation is achieved by modulating by major or minor thirds, avoiding the more traditional modulations in Western music and helping to create a distinctly Russian sound. Mussorgsky is often considered the most significant composer in characterizing the Russian style of the "Mighty Five."

31. C: The publisher is not an aspect of the score the conductor needs to learn when preparing a score; however, the form, transpositions, and dynamics of the score are all necessary aspects of the score to learn when preparing a score for rehearsals and performances.

32. C: This is Beethoven's famous melody from the first movement of his *Eroica Symphony No. 3* in Eb major. Shortly before composing this symphony, Beethoven went through an emotional crisis in his life, writing what has become known as the "Heiligenstadt Testament." This symphony is said to mark a change in Beethoven's writing, and it is a line of demarcation from writing in the Classical style to writing in a more Romantic style. It is characterized by a movement beyond traditional boundaries in form, length, harmony, and emotional expression.

33. B: To find the harmony of the chord, the pitches must be stacked in root position so that the note names are a third apart. In the given example, root position would be: A-C-Eb-G. Because the interval between the root and the fifth is a diminished 5th and the distance between the root and the seventh is minor 7th, the harmony of the given chord is A half-diminished 7th.

34. A: The chord in the given example is an E# diminished triad. In the key of F# major, this chord is built on the seventh scale degree of the F# major scale (F#-G#-A#-B-C#-D#-<u>E#</u>-F#). In standard music theory notation, the E# diminished chord can be written in Roman numerals as vii^{o}, answer A.

35. B: The gamelan ensemble is the traditional ensemble music of Javanese, Sundanese, and Balinese in Indonesia. The gamelan orchestra contains tuned percussion instruments like bells, gongs, drums, and metallophones. It is used for celebratory, religious, and political purposes.

36. A: If the pitch is lower than an F#, and assuming that the barrel and mouthpiece assembly are properly in place, the student should take less mouthpiece into the mouth, firm the corners of the embouchure, blow more air, or some combination of those three techniques. If the pitch is higher than an F#, the student should take more mouthpiece into the mouth, blow less air, or some combination of those two actions. The student should practice performing on the barrel and mouthpiece when first learning to play. Performing with the correct pitch ensures that the grip, angle of the mouthpiece, amount of air used (a fast stream), and the amount of mouthpiece taken into the mouth is correct.

37. A: The chord in the given example has G as its root, so that the chord in root position can be spelled: G-B-D-F#. Because the interval from G to F# is a major seventh, rather than a minor 7th, the chord is a major 7th chord. The 7th note of the chord—F#—is in the bass, which indicates that the chord is in third inversion, thus the correct answer is A: major seventh in third inversion.

38. B: Imitation is a foundational tool for beginning improvisation. Imitation allows students to learn techniques, progressions, melodic contour, and rhythmic patterns of improvisers of the past. Once students have immersed themselves in studying imitation, they will be much better suited to assimilate improvisation techniques for new musical ideas.

39. C: During a rehearsal, the director should periodically check for accurate intonation of the ensemble. Aside from beginning each rehearsal with accurate tuning, the director should isolate each different section for intonation spot checks. This teaches the students to listen attentively to themselves and also to the surrounding students.

40. D: A loud, forceful, and fast sound tends to convey passion, answer D. Sorrow tends to be represented by slower sounds; calm is usually represented by slower, light sounds; and hope tends to be represented by sustained, high sounds.

41. B: A tone cluster is defined as a group of closely spaced notes played simultaneously, usually in intervals of adjacent seconds and groupings, or "clusters." Extended harmony and a diminished seventh have notes that are spaced more widely than adjacent seconds, and retrograde inversion refers to twelve-tone music technique.

42. C: Hand-horn technique, also known as right hand technique, is the placement of the right hand inside the bell of the horn to produce a slightly darker tone, to more easily control pitch, and to perform extended techniques such as stopped horn and echo horn.

43. C: Double reed woodwind instruments produce sound when air is blown through two reeds that are tied together and vibrate. Double reed instruments include the oboe, bassoon, and sarrusophone. The clarinet is a single reed instrument, not a double reed instrument.

44. C: The *opera seria* that arose during the Enlightenment focused on tragic and serious subjects. The structure, number of singers, and plot line were structured so that the action usually took place in three acts with alternating arias and recitatives, and the number of characters usually numbered six or seven with two to four main characters.

45. B: A career in music business would include the job title of (B), publicist. Other related job titles are publisher, media promotion specialist, event promoter, arts writer, product manager, recording studio manager, artist scout, account executive, finance assistant, artist liaison, tour manager, booking agent, radio promoter, and music licensing supervisor.

Practice Test #3

1. Which of the following forms is a monothematic composition in which a single subject is continually echoed throughout the piece through imitation and development?

a. Fugue form
b. Strophic form
c. Sectional variation
d. Rondo form

2. What 1953 Broadway musical featured the following melody from Alexander Borodin's opera *Prince Igor* and was later covered by such pop stars as Tony Bennett, Johnny Mathis, and Nat King Cole?

a. *Carousel*
b. *Anything Goes*
c. *Damn Yankees*
d. *Kismet*

3. Which of the following improvisational tools is based on a dialogue structure?

a. Repetition
b. Question and answer
c. Syncopation
d. Heterophony

4. When an alto saxophone player begins to double on a Bb soprano clarinet, which of the following embouchure differences should be accounted for?

a. The lips should be pulled further back for the clarinet.
b. The mouthpiece should be taken in more for the clarinet.
c. The corners of the embouchure should be firmer for the clarinet.
d. The chin should be more pulled down and concave for the clarinet.

5. Which of the following major leaders in music education suggested that *a cappella* singing and native folk songs should be the primary means for children to gain music understanding?

a. Kodály
b. Gordon
c. Orff
d. Dalcroze

6. When arranging music, which group of instruments would best function as a crisp and bright fanfare?

a. Strings
b. Woodwinds
c. Low brasses
d. High brasses

7. Which of the following modern composers, along with Phillip Glass, helped pioneer the subgenre of minimalism in music?

a. John Cage
b. Francis Poulenc
c. Charles Ives
d. Bela Bartok

8. When performing the following music excerpt, which of the following is an area a conductor is most likely to have difficulty with?

(Stravinsky, *The Rite of Spring,* "The Sacrificial Dance")

a. Navigating the frequent changes in meter while maintaining flowing musicality
b. Maintaining the slow, grave tempo without rushing
c. Maintaining interest with simple textures and harmony
d. Adding grace notes to the various instrument parts

9. Which of the following differentiated instructional strategies is most practical when teaching guitar in a general music setting?

a. Separate high achievers from low achievers.
b. Eliminate individual formative assessments.
c. Provide each student with short personal lessons.
d. Design group projects based upon mutual interests.

10. What is the lower limit for a middle school male whose voice has already changed?

a. G3
b. F3
c. A3
d. D3

11. Which of the following compositional devices is used in the final measures of the following music excerpt?

(Chopin *Nocturne Op. 9,* No. 1 in Bb Minor Larghetto)

a. Whole-tone scale
b. Octatonic scale
c. Picardy third
d. Sequence

12. Which of the following slide adjustments is most likely to be used when adjusting for intonation on a Bb trumpet in the last measure of the music excerpt shown below?

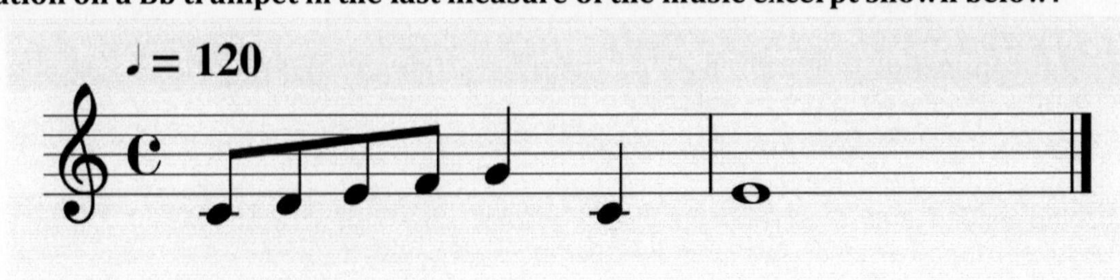

a. Pull out first and third slides
b. Push in first and third slides
c. Pull out first slide
d. Push in first slide

13. Which three Western music eras can best be described as the time when polyphonic music was developed and reached its peak use?

a. Medieval, Renaissance, Baroque
b. Baroque, Classical, Romantic
c. Classical, Romantic, Impressionist
d. Impressionist, Modern, Post-modern

14. Which of the following conducting patterns best fits the music excerpt?

(Elgar Enigma Variations VII Op. 36)

a.

b.

c.

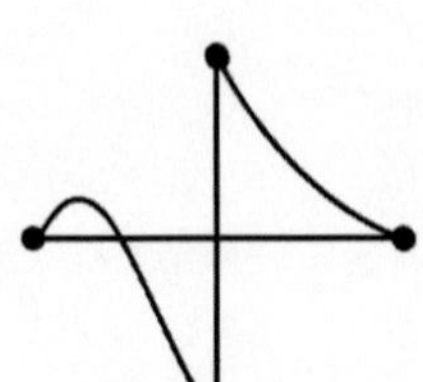

d.

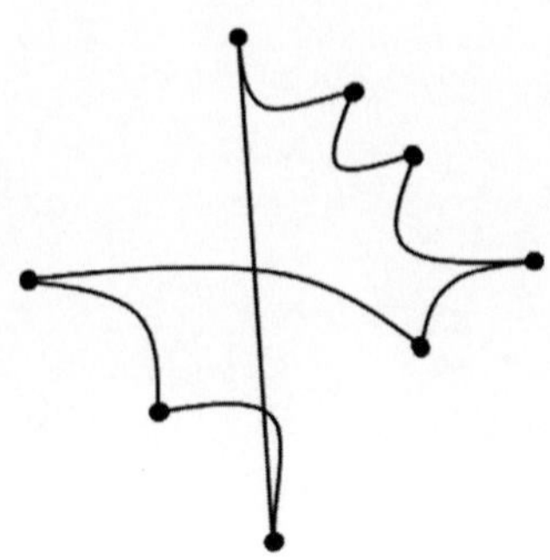

15. Which of the following vocal exercises helps a singer begin to learn how to perform a smooth transition through a vocal break?

a. Pushing air to support vocal folds
b. Humming warm-ups
c. Closing the mouth to help slow down air flow
d. Enunciation drills

16. Use the example below to answer the question that follows.

Which of the following best describes the above cadence?

a. Perfect authentic cadence
b. Plagal cadence
c. Deceptive cadence
d. Half cadence

17. Use the example below to answer the question that follows.

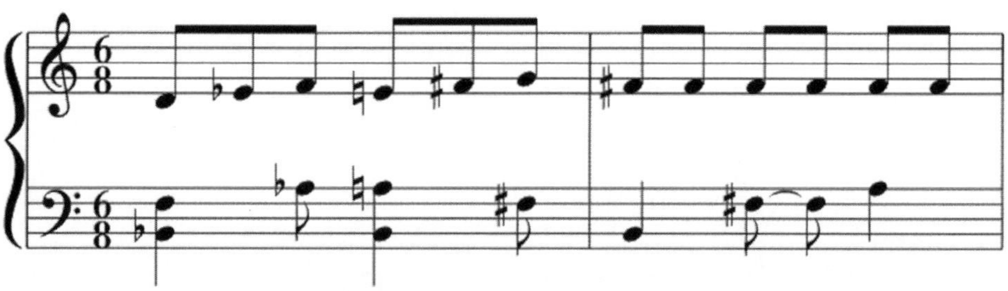

The second measure of the above example uses which rhythmic device?

a. Anacrusis
b. Horizontal hemiola
c. Suspension
d. Augmentation

18. Students pretend to pick up and drink a teacup filled with tea. Then, students pretend to pick up a teacup filled with liquid lead. Which of Laban's effort elements are most directly changed?

a. Weight and flow
b. Time and space
c. Weight and space
d. Time and flow

19. Which pop musician directly references the excerpt of this Chopin Prelude?

a. Stevie Wonder
b. Ray Charles
c. John Legend
d. Billy Joel

20. Which of the following "Mighty Five" compositional techniques is used in the following music excerpt?

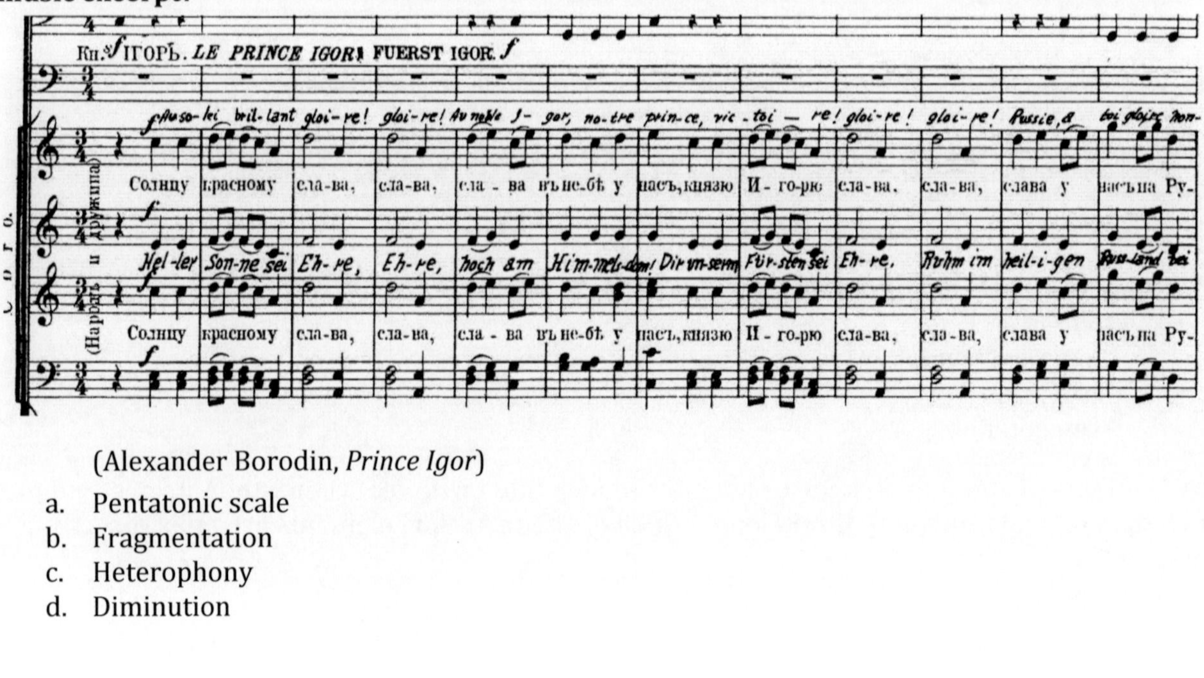

(Alexander Borodin, *Prince Igor*)

a. Pentatonic scale
b. Fragmentation
c. Heterophony
d. Diminution

21. Which of the following choral structures is the most common for four-part vocal harmony?

a. SATB
b. SAB
c. SSAA
d. TTBB

22. Which of the following software applications is commonly thought of as the industry standard for professional music notation?

a. MuseScore
b. GarageBand
c. Dorico
d. Cubase

23. What is the name of the highly useful digital interface that allows communication between digital instruments and computers, facilitating ease of composing, arranging, performing, recording, and editing?

a. RAM
b. DAW
c. MIDI
d. MP4

24. Use the example below to answer the question that follows.

Which of the following best describes the harmonic interval in the above example?

a. Augmented 7th
b. Minor 7th
c. Diminished 7th
d. Major 7th

25. Which of the following notation programs allows musicians to notate compositions electronically and then transfer the data to other MIDI instruments?

a. Mozarteum
b. Sibelius
c. MagicNote
d. Forte Score

26. For intermediate to advanced clarinet players, when tuning with a band or wind ensemble with concert Bb, which of the following clarinet tuning sequences is most appropriate for a clarinet player to use when tuning his or her instrument?

a. C4, C5
b. E3, E4
c. C5, G5
d. G3, E3

27. Which of the following musical terms most closely means "to perform at your pleasure" and without a strict tempo, as in a cadenza?

a. A Niente
b. A Battuta
c. A Piacere
d. A Cappella

28. Use the example below to answer the question that follows.

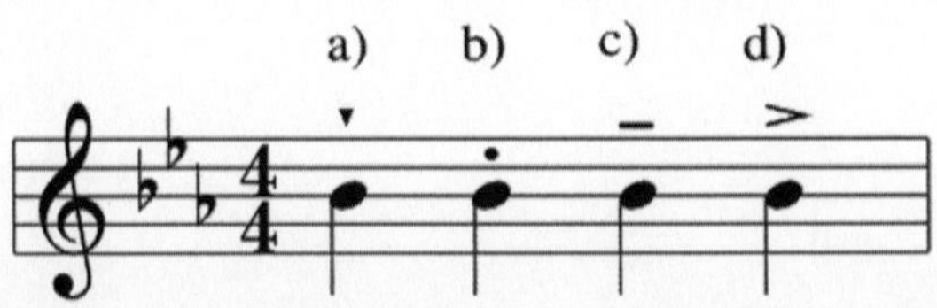

In the example, which articulation indicates that the note should be played with the shortest duration?

a. Staccatissimo
b. Staccato
c. Tenuto
d. Accent

29. The overtone series can be best understood within the context of which scientific discipline?

a. Chemistry
b. Biology
c. Physics
d. Astronomy

30. How does the hand move when conducting a 4/4 beat pattern?

a. Upward on the first beat, downward on the second beat, inward on the third beat, and outward on the fourth beat
b. Inward on the first beat, outward on the second beat, upward on the third beat, and downward on the fourth beat
c. Outward on the first beat, upward on the second beat, downward on the third beat, and inward on the fourth beat
d. Downward on the first beat, inward on the second beat, outward on the third beat, and upward on the fourth beat

31. Which of the following composers is MOST strongly associated with the Romantic Period?

a. Johann Sebastian Bach
b. Maurice Ravel
c. Aaron Copland
d. Johannes Brahms

32. What is one reason why there is a movement in lower elementary general music classes to replace teaching soprano recorder with ukulele?

a. The ukulele is an accompanying instrument
b. The ukulele sounds better in a group setting
c. The ukulele is easier to learn than the recorder
d. The ukulele is more culturally relevant in society

33. Use the example below to answer the question that follows.

Which of the following chord progressions best describes the above example?

a. ii$^{6}/_{4}$ – V – vi^{6} - iii
b. I^{6} – IV – V$^{6}/_{4}$ - ii
c. IV – V$^{6}/_{4}$ – I - ii
d. iii^{6} – V – I$^{6}/_{4}$ - IV

34. What is the main role of the free hand when conducting an ensemble?

a. Keeping the beat
b. Musical reinforcement
c. Balance
d. Following the score

35. When using a standard trigger on a Bb tenor trombone, which of the following intervals does the trigger expand the instrument's range by?

a. Lowers by a perfect fourth
b. Lowers by a perfect fifth
c. Raises by a major third
d. Raises by a perfect fifth

36. When adjusting levels for your microphone through a mixer on digital audio workstation software and an audio interface, which decibels relative to full scale (dBFS) level should your audio recording software peak at?

a. 0 dBFS
b. −3 dBFS
c. −6 dBFS
d. −12 dBFS

37. For music students, which of the following movement sequences should the Laban effort elements initially be taught with?

a. Space, weight, time, flow
b. Weight, time, space, flow
c. Time, flow, space, weight
d. Flow, space, weight, time

38. Cajun music of Louisiana traces its roots back to which European culture?

a. French
b. Dutch
c. Flemish
d. Portuguese

39. What is the top range of flute parts in published band music that is graded level I?

a. A5
b. C6
c. G5
d. D5

40. When a student memorizes common practice period rules, such as the four uses of the second inversion tonic chord, which of the following parts of Bloom's taxonomy is being most engaged?

a. Knowledge
b. Comprehension
c. Application
d. Analysis

41. Which of the following instructional strategies is the most practical technique to modify music instruction when teaching classical guitar in a general music classroom?

a. Separate high achievers from low achievers
b. Eliminate individual formative assessments
c. Provide each student with short personal lessons
d. Design group projects based upon mutual interests

42. Use the example below to answer the question that follows.

Identify the type of dissonance found above the asterisk in the given voice-leading example.

a. Neighbor tone
b. Suspension
c. Passing tone
d. Appoggiatura

43. The second motif of the first movement of this symphony, illustrated in the music excerpt below, begins with the cellos before moving to the upper strings. Musicians often refer to this symphony as the "symphony that ______ wrote but didn't finish." Which of the following composers wrote this symphony?

a. Schumann
b. Berlioz
c. Schubert
d. Mahler

44. What is the name of the motion of two musical lines where one line stays stationary while the other musical line moves in an upward or downward direction?

a. Contrary motion
b. Parallel motion
c. Similar motion
d. Oblique motion

45. Which of the following instruments is typically notated on the treble clef and sounds a minor third higher than written?

a. B♭ clarinet
b. A clarinet
c. D clarinet
d. E♭ clarinet

Answer Key and Explanations for Test #3

1. A: Of the answer choices, the fugue is a monothematic composition in which a single subject is continually echoed throughout the piece through imitation and development. The fugue theme is introduced at the beginning of the work, also known as the exposition, and is echoed in all of the fugal voices in different pitches and various keys.

2. D: The primary melody from the ballet *Polovtsian Dances* from Borodin's opera *Prince Igor* was used in the musical *Kismet* in 1953. The musical won a Tony award in 1954. The melody was used in the song titled "Stranger in Paradise."

3. B: The question and answer improvisational tool is based on dialogue structure. As in dialogue within language, there is interplay between speakers and lines: a musical line "responds" to a previous musical line, and this response can come from a different musician, instrument, group, or register within a solo performer.

4. C: Because the clarinet requires more air pressure to play (smaller aperture in the mouthpiece, smaller bore in the instrument), the embouchure must be firmer. This is accomplished by tightening the corners of the mouth.

5. A: Kodály used techniques from various music pedagogies, including Sarah Glover and John Curwen's hand signs and Émile-Jacques Dalcroze's emphasis on movement. However, he wished for all Hungarian children to become musical through the singing of folk songs of their mother country.

6. D: When arranging music, high brasses would best function as a crisp and bright fanfare. Fanfares are closely associated with brass instruments. Woodwinds lack the penetrating power of high brass, so they are not the best choice. Strings also are not as closely associated with fanfare and are not as bright as high brasses. Low brasses would not provide as bright a tone as high brasses.

7. A: John Cage was also known as an experimental composer. Characteristics of minimalism include fragmented melodies; slowly changing harmonic functions; complex counterpoints, and transformations of various types (textural, dynamic, melodic and rhythmic) over a period of time.

Francis Poulenc was a French composer and pianist of the early and mid-20th century. He was influenced by Debussy, Ravel, and Stravinsky, and seemed to reject serialism for music that was "easier to listen to." His later works were influenced by his growing seriousness and religious devotion.

8. A: This part of Igor Stravinsky's *The Rite of Spring*, first performed in Paris under the baton of Pierre Monteux in 1913, is considered extremely difficult to conduct because of the speed with which the metric changes take place. Conductors may struggle to navigate these changes while maintaining musicality. Option B is incorrect because this section does not have a slow tempo. Option C is incorrect because the textures and harmony of this section are complex. Option D is incorrect because the conductor does not add grace notes.

9. D: Option D is the correct answer because teachers can group by student preferences when offering choices of tunes or songs that students want to learn, such as learning about the history and use of the guitar in different cultural settings or genres and then having the different groups of students present their findings and perform to the rest of the class. Option A is incorrect because high and low achievers can both learn from one another (often more than they do from the teacher), even when differentiating instruction, such as progressing with tonal and rhythm patterns through Gordon's skill learning sequence, or when assigning students different tunes or songs to learn as homework in order to play for the class. Option B is incorrect because formative assessment assists the teacher in deciding how to differentiate instruction based upon achievement and preferences. Option C is incorrect because it is impractical to provide individual lessons to each student. A better option is to pair high achievers with low achievers for peer coaching.

10. D: The lower limit for a middle school male whose voice has already changed is D3. Although the voice has changed, it is still developing and will not have the range—or the strength and endurance—of a choral high school tenor or bass.

11. C: The Picardy third was used as early as the 15th to 17th centuries but also during the Romantic era. Chopin prepares for the Picardy third at the end of the music with falling thirds, setting up a dominant function, followed by the repetition of the Bb major tonic harmonic function at the end.

12. C: The written E is usually slightly sharp, particularly in the key of C, as shown in the question. Pulling a slide out lowers the pitch and pushing the slide in raises the pitch. Because the standard fingering of the E is first and second valves, there is no need to pull the third valve slide because there is no air going through that tubing and the pitch will not be affected. Additionally, the second valve slide on a trumpet does not have a mechanism allowing it to be pushed in or pulled out during performance (it is too small). Thus, the first valve slide is used solely to adjust the pitch.

The E shown in the first measure goes by too quickly for a player to typically need to adjust, as there is no time to do so and the note goes by too fast for there to be a noticeable problem with intonation.

13. A: Polyphonic music in the West is known to have primarily begun developing with melismatic organum during the Middle Ages, in which an ornate musical line was added above plainchant. Polyphony further developed during the Renaissance. Motets during the Renaissance developed to be more imitative than Medieval motets. During the Baroque period, polyphony became extremely complex and reached its apex of popularity. Options B, C, and D are incorrect because, although each music era contains polyphonic music, polyphonic music was primarily developed and reached its peak use during the Medieval, Renaissance, and Baroque eras.

14. B: Elgar (1857-1934) was an English composer who wrote *Enigma Variations* in 1899. The above excerpt is from variation seven and the tempo is *presto*. Because of the phrasing characteristics, one may be tempted to conduct the piece in 4/4 like Option C, however, the tempo of the music moves so that the appropriate pattern is a two-beat pattern. The music is not quite fast enough to warrant a one-beat pattern.

15. C: Closing the mouth slows down air flow and reduces air compression. Slowly singing downward through a closed mouth helps the singer to concentrate on making the sound pressure more evenly distributed throughout the register, which is the first step in smoothing out a break. Option A is incorrect because too much pushing with the air puts excess air compression on the vocal folds, exacerbating the break. Option B does not improve transitions through a vocal break as directly as option C. Option D trains enunciation, not transitions through a vocal break.

16. D: The open chords in the given example are Eb major, which is the I chord in the key, and Bb major, which is the V chord. Of the answer choices, the only cadence that ends on a V chord is answer D: half cadence. Perfect authentic cadences progress from V-I; plagal cadences, IV-I; and deceptive cadences, usually from V-VI.

17. B: Hemiola is a word that describes rhythms that are contrasted in a 3:2 ratio, most commonly exemplified by having 3 beats occupy the space that is ordinarily given 2 beats. In the given example, the treble notes shift from groupings of 3 to groupings of 2 in 6/8 meter, which gives a sense of meter change from triple to duple. This is an example of the less common form of hemiola known as horizontal hemiola. Anacrusis refers to notes before the downbeat of the first measure, suspension refers to voice leading within tonal harmony, and augmentation refers to rhythmic lengthening.

18. A: Weight and flow are most directly changed in this example. Laban's model related elements of bodily movement to creativity and described four continuums to taxonomize elements of motion. This was used to inspire creativity in students by having them experience paradoxical scenarios, such as "picking up a teacup filled with liquid lead." This causes the students to respond imaginatively to an unrealistic scenario. The continuums related to each of Laban's effort elements are:

FLOW
Bound - - - - - - - - - - - Free
SPACE
Direct - - - - - - - - - - - Indirect
WEIGHT
Heavy - - - - - - - - - - - Light
TIME
Slow - - - - - - - - - - - Fast

When changing the liquid in a pretend teacup from water to lead, the weight becomes heavier. This weight change makes the flow of the cup become more bound. The timing and the space are unaffected.

19. D: Billy Joel directly quotes from Chopin's Op. 28, No. 15 in Db major ("Raindrop") in his introduction to the song "Souvenir" on the ninth track of his album titled *Streetlife Serenade*.

20. A: The use of the pentatonic scale gave the "Mighty Five" another way to sound unique compared to Western music because the pentatonic scale conveys an impression of folk music and an Eastern origin.

21. A: The most common choral structure for four-part vocal harmony is SATB (soprano, alto, tenor, bass). SAB only makes use of three voices, and SSAA and TTBB are not as commonly used as SATB.

22. C: Options B and D are very popular digital audio workstations, and Option A is a popular open-source desktop music publishing application, but it is not as sophisticated as Dorico and is not the industry standard for professional music writing notation software. Ultimately, the difference in effectiveness may be dictated by features that are accessible, such as MIDI input functionality. Usually, paid software comes with more support and stronger features within the platform, however, students and teachers have access to satisfactory features through free-to-use software. For many years, *Finale* was the industry standard, but it is no longer available for sale as of 2024. Dorico has since taken a leading role in the professional space as Finale has declined.

23. C: MIDI is the name of the highly useful digital interface that allows communication between digital instruments and computers, facilitating ease of composing, arranging, performing, recording, and editing. Short for Musical Instrument Digital Interface, it does not record a digital version of a sound recording but instead stores performance data of a particular performance, such as key presses, velocity, and pedal movements.

24. B: The harmonic interval in the example shows G-flat to F-flat. In the major diatonic scale, the 7th interval from G-flat would be F. Because the 7th note is lowered by a half step, it is a minor 7th interval. An augmented 7th would be G-flat to F-sharp, and a diminished 7th would be G-flat to F-double flat.

25. B: Sibelius is notation software that allows musicians to notate compositions electronically and then transfer the data to other MIDI instruments. Other similar programs include MuseScore, Dorico, and Finale. Using notation software helps to reinforce musical concepts and compositional lessons for students.

26. A: The clarinet, when tuned to C4, is tuned with the barrel and first joint assembly. This joint affects not only the left-hand part of the clarinet, but also the tuning of the entire clarinet more than the middle joint and the bell joint, which are used to help tune the right-hand part of the clarinet. One tunes with the barrel and works their way down, understanding that there will always be some compromise among notes and between the top and bottom part of the clarinet. After tuning to the C4, players should tune to the C5—this tone has a natural tendency to play a little sharp. Pulling the middle joint can be used to place this tone in tune.

The significant point is to tune the left-hand first in a relatively in-tune part of the clarinet, then tune the right-hand in a relatively in-tune part of the clarinet.

When tuning to a concert A in an orchestra, some clarinet players prefer to tune to an F#4, then a B4. Another variation using the left hand is that some clarinet players prefer to start tuning with the open G4 instead of the C4, although the G4 usually has a natural tendency to play a little sharp.

The bell is used for right-hand pinky tones only.

27. C: *Piacere* means the performer is able to play as they please. *Niente* means to fade away to nothing. *Battuta* means to return to a normal tempo (*battuto* means to strike the strings on a stringed instrument with the bow). *Cappella* means to perform without instrumental accompaniment.

28. A: Of the answer choices, staccatissimo has the shortest duration. Staccato indicates that the note should be played short but not as short as staccatissimo. Tenuto indicates that the note should be played for its full length or slightly longer. Accent indicates that the note should be played with a strong stress.

29. C: The overtone series can be best understood within the context of physics, the study of matter and its motion through space and time. The concept of overtones refers to a specific acoustic property of sound. For every one frequency, there are multiple other frequencies, or overtones, that vibrate through the resonant space of its normal modes.

30. D: When conducting, the downbeat of the pattern always indicates the strongest pulse of the pattern and is indicated by a downward stroke of the hand. The last beat of the pattern is always the weakest pulse of the pattern and is thus indicated by an upward stroke of the hand. In a 4/4 pattern then, the hand moves downward on the first beat, inward on the second beat, outward on the third beat, and upward on the fourth beat.

31. D: Johannes Brahms composed music in the middle to late 19th century. Therefore, Brahms is most strongly associated with the Romantic Period in classical music, which ran from about 1815 to about 1910. Bach is most strongly associated with the Baroque Period (1600-1760), and Ravel is most closely associated with the Impressionist Period (1890-1940). Aaron Copland, often is considered "the dean of American composers" and composed music in the mid to late 20th century; he would not fit into any of the above listed periods.

32. A: Option A is correct because students can learn to accompany themselves while singing songs. Option B is incorrect because both the recorder and the ukulele can sound pleasant in group settings. (In particular, see Richard Grunow and Edwin Gordon's *Jump Right in: The Instrumental Series* for recorder. It teaches the recorder while also teaching audiation, which improves recorder performance.) Option C is incorrect because this is a subjective rationale: there has been little or no published objective experimental research that justifies this statement. Option D is incorrect because both the ukulele and the soprano recorder can be used in an Orff Instrumentarium. The recorder has a long history in Western European music, beginning in the Middle Ages, and continues to be popular throughout the country and in American culture.

33. B: The chords in the example are E major in first inversion, A major in root position, B major in second inversion, and F# minor in root position. In the key of E major, the chords given should be written in Roman numerals relative to their scale degrees in the key (<u>E</u>-<u>F#</u>-G#-<u>A</u>-<u>B</u>-C#-D#): I^6 – IV – V$^6/_4$ – ii.

34. B: The main role of the free hand when conducting an ensemble is as musical reinforcement. As an independent stimulus, the free hand can reinforce dynamics such as crescendos and decrescendos as well as aid in cueing parts. The free hand should also indicate releases, phrasing, musical style, and necessary modifications in the balance of the ensemble.

35. A: Depressing the trigger opens up additional tubing. The principle is that the bigger the instrument, the lower the sound. When using the trigger, the lowest fundamental pitch on the instrument goes from Bb to F.

36. C: In digital workstations, the maximum dBFS is 0. Anything above 0 dBFS will clip and cause issues such as distortion or loss of signal; therefore, it is best to leave some room for adjustment of levels and aim for around –6 dBFS. While lower peak levels are still usable, aiming for around –6 dBFS is a common practice.

37. D: Movement instruction, according to Laban and others, should always begin with flow. Gordon advocated beginning with non-locomotor continuous fluid motion in order to promote audiation. When music students rush a tempo, they are displacing their weight through time and space. Planning and moving over an extended period of time improves a student's sense of timing, rhythm, and expression. An excellent experience for elementary music students is to sing the song made famous by Peggy Lee, composed by Arthur Hamilton, titled *The Rainbow Song*. Students can raise their arms above their heads, holding a colored scarf in each hand, and move their arms side to side, striving to reach the end point of each side at exactly the end of each phrase of the song.

38. A: Cajun music of Louisiana traces its roots back to French musical traditions. Early French settlers on the North American continent migrated from New Brunswick and Nova Scotia to southern Louisiana and brought with them traditional French ballads that, over time, developed into present-day Cajun music.

39. B: In published band music that is graded level I, C6 is the top range of flute parts. Some beginning flute players, particularly audiators, can use their right-hand pinky finger to perform down to a low C4 and even up to a high G6. Students who use multiple methods, one being a method that teaches audiation (e.g., *Jump Right In: The Instrumental Series*) and the other being a standard lesson book, actually tend to move more quickly through the lesson book, particularly if they are students who have at least average music aptitude. Students with low music aptitude move more slowly through the audiation-based method book and, hence, also through the standard lesson book. To be clear, achievement in audiation and in playing songs by rote and by ear in multiple keys and tonalities drive the executive (technical) skills required to move through standard lesson books. State and local performance standards reflect or are a reflection of published instrument and vocal ranges for every instrument and voice type. In establishing minimum standards, a maximum standard for most students is also established, thus protecting players from bad performance habits or physical harm by extending a range beyond what is physically reasonable.

40. A: Memorizing common practice period rules is recall of information. Option B is incorrect because comprehension is about understanding the meaning, translation, interpolation, and interpretation of instructions and problems. A student that can state a problem in their own words shows comprehension. Option C is incorrect because application is when a student uses a taught concept in a new situation, an unprompted use of an abstraction, in the classroom, or from readings during novel situations. Option D is incorrect because analysis is what happens when a student separates material or concepts into component parts so that the organizational structures may be understood (an extension of application). A student that distinguishes between facts and inferences shows analysis.

41. D: Option D is the correct answer because teachers can group by student preferences when offering choices of tunes or songs that students want to learn, learning about the history and use of the guitar in different cultural settings or genres, and then having the different groups of students present their findings and perform to the rest of the class, etc. Option A is incorrect because high and low achievers learn from one another (often more than they do from the teacher), even when differentiating instruction, such as progressing with tonal and rhythm patterns through Gordon's skill learning sequence, or when assigning students different tunes or songs to learn as homework in order to play for the class, etc. Option B is incorrect because formative assessment assists the teacher in deciding how to differentiate instruction based upon achievement and preferences. Option C is incorrect because it is impractical to provide individual lessons to each student. A better option is to pair high achievers with low achievers for peer coaching.

42. C: The F# dissonance in the given example comes between a G and E, so that the soprano line moves downwards in a step-wise motion. This is an example of a passing tone. A neighbor tone also moves in a stepwise motion but returns to the original tone; a suspension sounds on a downbeat, then moves downward by step; and an appoggiatura is a leap followed by a step.

43. C: This is Schubert's *Symphony No. 8*, D759 in B minor. Schubert is often regarded as a link between the Classical and Romantic eras. Schumann wrote four Romantic symphonies. The French composer Hector Berlioz wrote four Romantic symphonies, his most famous being *Symphonie fantastique*. Mahler wrote ten symphonies, characterizing the height of the Romantic era.

44. D: Oblique motion refers to the motion of two musical lines in which one line stays stationary while the other musical line moves in an upward or downward direction. Contrary motion moves in opposite directions, parallel motion moves in the same direction, and similar motion refers to the motion of two musical lines that move in similar directions.

45. D: The E^b clarinet is typically notated on the treble clef and sounds a minor third higher than written. The B^b clarinet sounds a major second lower than written; the A clarinet sounds a minor third lower than written; and the D clarinet sounds a major second higher than written, all with a range of E3-C7.